AF395052

Do You Come From Gomorrah?

Born in Donegal, Frank McGuinness lives in Dublin and is Professor Emeritus in Creative Writing at University College Dublin. His plays include *The Factory Girls* (1982), *Baglady* (1985), *Observe the Sons of Ulster Marching Towards the Somme* (1985), *Innocence* (1986), *Carthaginians* (1988), *Mary and Lizzie* (1989), *The Bread Man* (1991), *Someone Who'll Watch Over Me* (1992), *The Bird Sanctuary* (1994), *Mutabilitie* (1997), *Dolly West's Kitchen* (1999), *Gates of Gold* (2002), *Speaking Like Magpies* (2005), *There Came a Gypsy Riding* (2007), *Greta Garbo Came to Donegal* (2010), *The Match Box* (2012), *The Hanging Gardens* (2013), *The Visiting Hour* (2021) and *Dinner With Groucho* (2022). Among his many widely staged versions are *Rosmersholm* (1987), *Peer Gynt* (1988), *Hedda Gabler* (1994), *A Doll's House* (1997), *The Lady from the Sea* (2008), *Oedipus* (2008), *Helen* (2009), *Ghosts* (2010), *John Gabriel Borkman* (2010), *Damned by Despair* (2012), *The Dead* (2012) and *Tartuffe* (2023).

by the same author

GATES OF GOLD
DOLLY WEST'S KITCHEN
MARY AND LIZZIE
SOMEONE WHO'LL WATCH OVER ME
MUTABILITIE
OBSERVE THE SONS OF ULSTER MARCHING TOWARDS THE SOMME
SPEAKING LIKE MAGPIES
THERE CAME A GYPSY RIDING
GRETA GARBO CAME TO DONEGAL
THE MATCH BOX
THE HANGING GARDENS
THE VISITING HOUR
DINNER WITH GROUCHO

FRANK MCGUINNESS PLAYS ONE
(*The Factory Girls, Observe the Sons of Ulster Marching Towards the Somme,
Innocence, Carthaginians, Baglady*)

FRANK MCGUINNESS PLAYS TWO
(*Mary and Lizzie, Someone Who'll Watch Over Me,
Dolly West's Kitchen, The Bird Sanctuary*)

translations and adaptations
A DOLL'S HOUSE (Ibsen)
PEER GYNT (Ibsen)
ELECTRA (Sophocles)
OEDIPUS (Sophocles)
THE STORM (Ostrovsky)
HECUBA (Euripides)
MISS JULIE (Strindberg)
PHAEDRA (Racine)
THE LADY FROM THE SEA (Ibsen)
HELEN (Euripides)
GHOSTS (Ibsen)
JOHN GABRIEL BORKMAN (Ibsen)
DAMNED BY DESPAIR (Tirso de Molina)
THE DEAD (Joyce)
TARTUFFE (Molière)

screenplays
Brian Friel's DANCING AT LUGHNASA

musicals
DONEGAL (with Kevin Doherty)

THE DAZZLING DARK: NEW IRISH PLAYS
(edited by Frank McGuinness)

FRANK McGUINNESS

Do You Come From Gomorrah?

faber

First published in 2026
by Faber and Faber Limited
The Bindery, 51 Hatton Garden
London, EC1N 8HN

Typeset by Brighton Gray
Printed and bound in the UK by CPI Group (Ltd), Croydon CR0 4YY

All rights reserved
© Frank McGuinness, 2026
Introduction © Graham Price, 2026

Frank McGuinness is hereby identified as author
of this work in accordance with Section 77 of the
Copyright, Designs and Patents Act 1988

All rights whatsoever in this work, amateur or professional,
are strictly reserved. Applications for permission for any use
whatsoever including performance rights must be made in
advance, prior to any such proposed use,
Casarotto Ramsay & Associates Limited, 3rd Floor,
7 Savoy Court, Strand, London, WC2R 0EX

No performance may be given unless a licence
has first been obtained

A CIP record for this book
is available from the British Library

ISBN 978–0–571–40489–6

Printed and bound in the UK on FSC® certified paper in line with our continuing
commitment to ethical business practices, sustainability and the environment
For further information see faber.co.uk/environmental-policy

Our authorised representative in the EU for product safety is
Easy Access System Europe, Mustamäe tee 50, 10621 Tallinn, Estonia
gpsr.requests@easproject.com

2 4 6 8 10 9 7 5 3

Introduction

Frank McGuinness's *Do You Come From Gomorrah?* is the first 'monologue play' that McGuinness has written since *The Match Box* in 2012. There are many distinguished examples of monologue plays in the history of modern Irish drama, such as Samuel Beckett's *Not I* (1972), Brian Friel's *Faith Healer* (1979) and Marina Carr's *iGirl* (2021). The first play of McGuinness's to utilise the dramatic form of monologue throughout the entirety of its length was *Baglady* in 1985. His most famous theatrical work, *Observe the Sons of Ulster Marching Towards the Somme* (1985), begins and ends with monologues delivered by the main character, Pyper.

What all McGuinness's monologists have in common (including the character in *Do You Come From Gomorrah?*) is they each feel compelled to deliver their identifying stories as a means of bearing witness to their trauma and sometimes those of other people who are no longer alive. In this respect, they often fulfil a comparable role to that of Horatio in *Hamlet*, who is commanded to dedicate his life to the telling of Hamlet's story because death is preventing him from doing so himself. By not giving the monologist in *Do You Come From Gomorrah?* a name, the drama implies that his identity is fluid as opposed to static and also that it is subordinated to a narrative that is broader than just his life story.

Do You Come From Gomorrah? relates the story of a young man who was a resident in a fictitious (Protestant/ Unionist-run) boys' home in Northern Ireland. Like many of the young inmates in this institution, he was sexually abused by members of the security forces. In an era in Irish history when the country is still rightly in shock because of the revelations of abuse of young people by Catholic clergy, *Do You Come From Gomorrah?* reminds its audience of how equally appalling sexual crimes were committed by those of other professions and religious persuasions on the island of Ireland. (Any similarity to real people or actual events is purely coincidental.) This is not to deny the appalling crimes done by servants of the Catholic Church but to allow for a broadening out of the narrative of the abuse suffered by young Irish and/ or British throughout all the provinces of Ireland over a long number of years.

The word 'Gomorrah' in the play's title can be said to symbolise the guilt that should be felt by the perpetrators of abuse but also of that silently forced upon the monologuist and others like him who felt the stirring of same-sex desire in Ireland at the time the play is set. All the thematic and dramaturgic elements that are present in *Do You Come From Gomorrah?* combine to mark it out as another notable example of modern and contemporary Irish drama's 'theatre of remembrance and commemoration'.

Graham Price
March 2026

Do You Come From Gomorrah? was first performed at the Abbey Theatre, Dublin, on 10 April 2026, with the following cast:

Man Ryan Donaldson

Director Sarah Baxter
Set and Costume Designer Alyson Cummins
Lighting Designer Sinéad McKenna
Composer Tom Lane
Sound Designer Martha Knight
Voice Director Andrea Ainsworth
Casting Director Barry Coyle
Assistant Set and Costume Designer Mar Parés Baraldés

For Marianne Faithfull,
for the songs, the shocks, the friendship

The speaker is a young man,
with a Northern Irish accent.

DO YOU COME FROM GOMORRAH?

I.

Music.

What's up with you, son?

I can't stick that question.

It reminds me of my ma before she goes bananas and I know the poor bitch is going that way and we're in for a hell of a hard time.

I try to tell her, I say, Mammy, calm down, there's no need to go bananas. She laughs.

She says, would you listen to him? He's calling his mother a monkey. He thinks I have filthy fleas. I should be eating bananas. Well, I'll put a smile on the other side of your face. You think it funny to insult your mother? You compare her to an animal. Is that how you see me? I know different. I am a beautiful zebra. Jesus, I am – then you are right. My clever son's found me out. A zebra – I belong to Africa. I am black and white, I am fucking dynamite. How did that happen – how the hell – it must have been when I gave birth to you.

Mammy, I'm white, the two of us are white.

She grabs my face, she kisses me in the mouth, she calls me by a name, she says, you're Michelle.

Mammy, I'm a boy. Michelle is a girl's name.

Where in fuck did you get that red hair?

I have black hair, Ma, why do you think it's red?

3

Because your father set fire to me. When he fucked me he struck a match and threw it at me. He left me then to burn to death.

I knew then it was time to hide in the garden. The stupid bitch would be certain to try to torch us in our beds. God love her, she would wake us up crying, bursting out crying, getting me out of the house, saying, I'm wild sorry, but do you see me? I am black, I am white, I am red all over – what am I? I am –

You are a sunburnt zebra, Ma, that's what you are.

She laughed. She said he's got it. He is the answer to my riddle. Sunburnt. A zebra. She went away and I was put in the place. The home on the hill. A refuge for wayward boys.

Is that the polite word for us? The less polite call us boys of working age, boys who come from abusive home lives. Who are they to say so? Well, that's where the courts put us for our own protection. Isn't that a bit of a laugh? Here we resided less like a school than you'd think, free enough to come and go, listening to readings each morning before breakfast from the good book, a choice of testaments, Old and New. Jesus, the dirtbags that boss us here, the wardens, the assistant wardens – what are they cut from? Shit, I'd say, but keep it quiet, because if word reached the ears of himself, the glorious leader, Beastie Billy himself – who can say what trouble's in store? You might never leave the home on the hill. Or if you do, it will be in a box and lie long forgotten, for he has friends all over the place, friends in high places, very high places. He'll soon let you know who and where, but I'm like that – trustworthy, saying nothing that's not necessary, capable of keeping my lips sealed. I'm that secretive I won't even whisper its name, should you ever ask me – ask me anything. I can assure you – you'll get nothing from me.

That's the way we're trained. You might not expect that we should be able to hold our tongues. But we can. We can.

2.

Music.

That's why I do best what the home on the hill expects me to do. Play dumb. I cannot answer your question about what happened. I don't remember.

I do not like the past. It is not kind to me. It does not belong to me. My clothes belong to me – Don't try to take them.

I wear what Ma gave me. I have a T-shirt, trousers, two socks, two trainers. That's all I'm wearing. I don't like you wondering if there's anything else.

That's my business, my mother's. They're my own clothes. I can change out of them if I choose to. I don't choose to. I own every stitch on my back and on every other part of me.

My T-shirt is a blue one. It is clean as clean can be. My socks are blue as well. My trainers are ridiculously expensive. They cost more than my ma's week's wages. That is how I know they are proof, fucking proof she loves me. She would spend every penny to get me the shoes I want to wear. I have only to ask. She obliges. How does she get the money? That's my business. I put

5

my hand in my pocket. And I pull out of it – what do
I pull out? Why do you need to know? It will cost you.
Have you cash? I only deal in cash. That's the way I do
business. Keep your hand out of my pockets.

My trousers are my own business. I'm a growing boy.
I have loads of pairs to change in case they start to smell.
I don't like the stink of dirty trousers. Ma hates it as well.
Sometimes when she's not herself she would barge into
the room – my room – she would barge in and she would
say, I am going to wash you – sweat and shit staining you,
every dirty, desperate stain – every sorrowful inch of your
father. And he's left you. Left us. What are we to do now?

She'd start to cry.

I would stop pretending to be asleep. I'd put my arms
round her. I'd say, Ma, it's all right, you have a good cry
if you want to.

That is when she'd break wind. Break wind like a volley
of shots. Sour the air like a million stink bombs. She'd
grab me in her arms. She'd shout. Fuck them, fuck them
all, we can still smell this joint out. Free the wind.

She'd sing, the wind, the wind is blowing, through the
graves the wind is blowing, freedom soon will come,
then we will come from the shadows.

She'd stop and shout, what am I doing singing a Fenian
song?

Ma, that's not Fenian – that's Leonard Cohen –

That's right, son, she'd say and she would be silent
and sit down. She'd never finish the song. Neither
can I. I'm a Protestant. We don't sing. We don't drink.
Well, we do but we deny it. That's what all good boys

do. Deny everything. And I tell you, there's nothing but good boys about here. The master, the glorious leader, Beastie Billy, makes sure of that. He has two rules he learned from the Reverend Doctor. Deny everything and do as the Reverend tells you. Trust him – he knows what's good for us all. I have to laugh when I hear the Big Man bellowing that roar, I know nothing about homosexuals, I know nothing about homosexuals. I know nothing about what went on in that home. Of course he knew – he knew everything. About Gomorrah. That's what we'll call this place. This institution. That's the name it deserves. Something nice and biblical, to show our respect for our faith, in the good book and all who preach it. Beastie Billy, he is with the man himself all the way. Delivering sermons, delighting the devout of the Free Presbyterians, assuring them on all the good work conducted in Gomorrah. Reforming our souls. Saving us from sin. Making sure we do our bit for Queen and Country. Drilling us to do our duty. And what is our greatest duty? To serve, you might say. To cater. And it's fair to say we do cater – we deal with – how do I say this – our clients like you to be clean and obedient and thin – to do as you are told – no fuss. Yes, we serve the forces. All branches, all bidding for our wares. You couldn't count them on the creases of one cock. Tired, dry, old cocks. Our buyers range up to the rank of major. Men who know how to behave. Men with exquisite manners. Men who matter in the military. Don't forget that. Men. Our men. Even beautiful men. Men who'd hold your one hand while your other slits your throat. Not that this happened. Nothing whatsoever happened. We'd all swear to that – boys and men. Big and small men, ugly and handsome men, all shapes and stripes, sellers and buyers.

Music.

And I have never seen a more handsome man. Thank
Christ he has not arrived in gorgeous uniform or
I would not be able to control myself. British soldier's
uniform. No, he's not a major, but he's high up in the
ranks.

I want this soldier – he's called Steve, perfect Steve –
I want this Steve to be my friend, my fucker, my fella.
I want to suck the buttons of his navy blazer. I want to
unlace the black shoes on his white feet. I want to strip
them bare and kiss each and every one of his long toes.
I want to bathe the same feet in seasalt water, so I could
suck the tang of the ocean from his flesh.

Beastie Billy pats me on the head. He tells me – he
asks me, well, was he worth waiting for? Was the
agony in the gateway worth it? Enduring the slow
juices of Fermanagh's farmers. The scratches of Antrim
bachelors, listening to them doubting if the North
would survive, asking me to pretend I'm a Fenian
bastard who wants to strip them of their land and
cattle, roast them in the Romanish fires of hell, scald
them with holy water or some other rubbish, force them
to kiss pictures of the Blessed Virgin and leave their lips
ablaze like hot coals. No more of that shit.

I toss aside all bibles to lower Steve's marvellous
trousers and I will drink him dry till he'll scream
with pleasure. He does not do so. I am shocked. He
retaliates by grabbing me by the curls of my jet black
hair. He sticks his tongue into my mouth. I hear him,
unmistakable, cry out, come on, Irish boy, sing to me,

sing. Danny Boy, that will do. That song – I love it, it brings a little tear to my eye. But if you come, and all the flowers are dying – and I am dead, as dead I well may be. So sad – isn't it? Sing to me, Paddy, sing.

As a good British lad, how can I point out there has been an error? I watch the panic on Beastie Billy's face. He too has realised, nobody can trust the English in the North of Ireland. Dear Jesus, has this fool come to the wrong whorehouse? I do think he has. Steve starts to laugh at the mistake. My gorgeous darling actually loves Catholics. He's had some before now. He assures me they do turn over after much strange persuasion, but they do prefer to treat an English guy as the passive partner. This my soldier friend finds particularly inviting. He can pretend the boy pretends –

Jesus, I cannot keep pretending. I want to cut to the chase. I need to know for sure, sooner rather than later. Do you want to ride me, Steven? I am hungry and I am desperate and I need to be fucked.

He smiles, he asks if I am married?

I tell him I can be, if that is what he likes.

4.

Music.

Jesus, my bloody luck, can you believe it? Is this not typical? Is this not wicked? Who would credit it?

Just when I thought I'd never see a finer man than Steve, there is another more than his equal standing in the kitchen of the home on the hill, yes, here in glamorous Gomorrah, peeling carrots, his cheekbones so beautiful I have to close my eyes in case he blinds me, his black, black hair, a touch of purple on his cheek and his mouth is tight, his chin is hard. I can barely breathe with shock at the sight of him. He knows the way I'm looking at him I want to be looked at back.

Do you know what time it is? That's what he asks me.

It's coming up to twelve o'clock, I say to him. We'd better get these peeled if they're to cook in time for the dinner. You stick to the carrots, I'll do the spuds. Are you the chef in these parts? he asks.

I just lend a hand – like everyone else, we have to pull our weight, I tell him. So you're a dab hand getting the grub? A beautiful cook. Can you do anything else about the house? he smiles. What else did your ma teach you?

To be a good boy, I say.

Are you always that? he wants to know.

I do my best to be, I tease him, I have very few complaints.

He looks at my watch.

Where did you get that from?

It was a present.

From a friend, or from Mammy and Daddy? he wants to discover.

A friend, I lie.

A special friend?

You could say that. I lower my voice.

Jesus, he must have fancied you to get that from him.
It didn't come cheap. What did you let him do to you?
Will you be sore for a month?

I laugh back at him. I say, no, but he might be.

He starts to chop the carrots with a sharp knife. The
sheer speed of him. The blade glistens against the
orange carrot, dicing perfectly what he's cut. You're
taking your time with those spuds, he accuses me. Will
you have them ready before Christmas?

I might, I laugh, you can have them as your present.

That's the difference between me and you, he says,
I never take presents from strangers.

Why not? I challenge him.

You never know what they might ask for back.

Not me, I assure you, I expect nothing in return.

Keep doing that, life won't let you down then, will it?
he said. So who do I have to humour in this kip? Is it
the ugly little bastard with the black rimmed glasses
with a look on his fat face like a bucket of vomit?

Beastie Billy we call him, for badness, I let him know,
he's a short wee dose, and he has hands that cover a
multitude of sins.

I know his type, passing on all he's picked up at Sunday
school, making sure we say our prayers while he unzips
us, am I right? he asks me.

Do as he asks, and he won't take a bite out of you,
I answer, but his pals might, he has friends in dangerous
places.

Don't we all? he lets me know.

No, not me, I confess, what's your name anyway?

He says it's Keith.

I've always liked that name but I say nothing in case he thinks I'm a soft touch and might believe he could make a few bob before the day's out. I know a fast worker when I see one.

How long have you been here? I ask him instead.

In Gomorrah? he says, I've just arrived. Sent here for being a bad boy. Difficult around girls. Don't look too disappointed. Surely you must have realised a bull like myself could not be trusted with the ladies. Does that shatter you? Will we not now become best friends? Why have you gone quiet? Why have you a long face? Have you no liking for girls? Are you frightened of them? You should be, you know. Belfast birds, they'd bite your balls off. Always be prepared to defend the honour of Ulster men. Do you know what I do to protect myself from the temptation of the fair sex and their campaign to corrupt our pure and noble menfolk?

What do you do? I ask him.

As I said, I'm a dangerous man about the women. But only if they're wearing frocks. Then I grab them and pull down their knickers. I cannot wait to put them on. I should have stuck to washing lines, but it's not the same buzz, Keith tells me, and then doesn't he burst out laughing? You believe me, don't you? he challenges.

Yes, I do believe you, I say.

Why? he asks.

They'd suit you, knickers, I tell him.

Someday I'll let you see me in them, he promises.

When? Where? I wonder to myself.

When we can slip away from here, he says, somewhere
more private, sometime when I can take you home,
introduce my family. I'm sure they'd take a shine to
you. A nice queer like yourself.

He said it – queer. And he continued to stand his
ground in front of me. Not slapping me. Not mocking.
Telling me he had a weekend pass. Come home, meet
his father. And I did.

5.

Music.

Keith's father scares the shite out of me.

I should have smelt a rat. Keith says to me, all I want
you to do is meet my father. You don't know yours too
well, but I do know mine. Is it that much to say hello to
him? For fuck's sake, I'm only asking you to just shake
his hand.

We pass through hell and high water to get into the
excuse for a pub where Papa Keith reigns supreme.
The funny thing is the kip is spotless, carpets, glasses,
ashtrays. The guy in charge prides himself on running
a shipshape organisation. Anything less would be a
slur on the Association and those who run it. In the
mornings I'd say the stench of Dettol would knock a
body out, that's how particular they are when it comes
to hygiene. There's never any evidence of anything

ever spilt here. A clean establishment, impeccably clean. Not too sure the same can be claimed by those drinking here, some of them almost swallowed by the tattoos. Keith's da has an orange rose painted on his biceps. A lovely large tarantula decorates his right arm, bared for the world to admire. They said nothing to each other for a wee while, then they nod. Are you still a nancy boy, or have you straightened yourself out? Daddy wants to know. Keith doesn't answer straight away – lets the insult run off him like water from a duck's back. Keith just says, Da, here's a mate, you've not set eyes before on him, and then the da turns his face to me, I know the bastard hates me because I want his son.

Keith decides to be all nice and noble. Shake hands with Da, he says, he just wants to shake hands. Do that for me. Go on, do it. Pay no heed to his bad-mouthing us. It's his nature. His way of having fun.

His da continues smoking. He lifts the cigarette to his mouth. He blows violet smoke into the air. He eyes me up and down. Is he going to spit in my face? No. He raises the cigarette to me. He holds it out in my direction. I don't know if he wants me to lift it and have a drag. He flashes it in my direction. All hands in the bar are eyeing me. Will I have the nerve to refuse? I shock the lot of them who have me down as another of Keith's cissies.

I decide to have nothing to do with this dirty habit. He is not upset. Instead he offers me another limb to shake. It is not a hand. It is a hook. Onto the hook he presses the burning fag. It is extinguished. He lets it drop to the ground. He makes sure it is out by stamping on the remains with his boot. I am frightened by him. He knows that. No point continuing to deny it.

I know who you are, the barman tells me, I know where you're residing, I know the wee favours you lads perform. There's a time and place for that carry-on, but not here, do you follow that?

He'd better, Keith's da says.

I follow – I follow clearly, I say, fucked if I'm letting the side down, though the shite might be shaking inside me.

Take him home, Daddy says to Keith. Enjoy the silly little bastard. There's word he's done his bit for us. You know where you can take him.

We can go to the house? Keith asks.

You can hardly do it on the town street, can you? Do you want to be the talk of Lisburn? Like my mother? Keith sneers.

Let sleeping dogs lie, his da says, and she's in a drunken coma somewhere. She'll hardly disturb you.

So we walk to where Keith lives.

I am led upstairs in Keith's family house.

He points to a bed, his parents' bed.

This is where he conceived me, that man with the hooked hand, Keith laughs, and so do I, excited as fuck. At long last, at long last . . .

6.

Music.

We're inside sitting round the table.

Keith's dad made us tea and toast. We're drinking and eating the lovely crusty brown bread, baked a few doors away, fresh out of the oven, smelling like Keith, his arms wrapped round me in the bed we've just left.

Tell us, Da, Keith said, how you got the hook instead of the hand.

It's all to do with the time I was driving a taxi, he says. I got this fare in the middle of Belfast and he asked me to drive him to Larne. It was late in the night, yet I agreed, even though it's a fair few miles, but I'd make a right amount of readies doing this run, so I said all right. Did I mention he was a Derry man, trying to get to Larne? As a rule, I have no fear of foreigners, except the culprits from Cork or Dublin, hell's gates to them and all who hail from those godless parts. So your man got into the car and he sat beside me. He was quite a big fellow, not fat at all but full of muscles – he could hold his own in a fight – and he says to me what do you do on your nights off?

What did you answer him? I asked Keith's da.

I didn't answer him. I kept my mouth shut. Next thing I know the Derry fella produced a noggin of dark rum, Jamaican, he opens it, takes a swig and offers me a drop. I don't take a blind bit of notice. Years of driving other people at their convenience have taught me how to keep my eyes steady on the road, let them get up to all kinds of shenanigans on the back seat, no concern of mine. Then he takes out of his trousers pocket –

You'll never guess this, Keith says, guess what it was.

You've already told him he'll never guess, and he won't.
He took out a woman's silver comb – a jewelled comb
with wee red rubies, and he went to comb my hair. In
the shock of a man touching me I lost control of the
car, and it crashed into a wall. I never saw as much
blood – that was when I lost fear at the sight of it.
The Derry man was killed instantly. I was left nearly
unmarked apart from my hand that went through the
windscreen and was severed because I was trying to
punch him away from me. The Lord alone knows where
his pawing me would have stopped. He lost his life and
I lost my hand. I warn you, boys, never give people lifts.
Picking people up – not the wisest of moves.

But you were driving a taxi, I point out, you have to
pick people up.

He was carrying an offensive weapon, Keith's da
retorts, so I was a fool to trust him. It was a comb he
was carrying – what happened to it?

Keith takes the jewelled comb out of his trousers
pocket. He says, I carry it with me always. I use it when
I fight bad boys. I have to flash it in case somebody calls
me a poof.

All through this conversation Keith's da was chewing
toast. Him and Keith burst out laughing at the word
poof. Then the old boy had more toast. He chewed and
chewed, never seeming to swallow.

7

Music.

Beastie Billy is on the warpath, so that means he's on the prowl, and that should scare the daylights out of everybody, as he could pounce on anyone unfortunate enough to catch his eye. He says they're sniffing around us, they're getting close. He says someone in this home must be squealing. He is getting phone calls from people who work for the papers, especially the fucking Dublin papers. They know things they shouldn't know. Names they shouldn't be able to name. It has to be coming from an inside source. We need to name the enemy. Why is he looking at Keith? Keith just keeps on looking back straight at him, and asks who is the enemy exactly?

This is the cue for Billy to start his sermon. He begins by telling us the enemy is strong and great. We must face down the forces of Romanism and Communism. We must be men of conviction, men of high principle, men of courage and faith prepared to resist to the death, if necessary, every attempt from whatever source to unfurl the banner of the Evil One – Remind me again, Keith interrupts him, who are the Evil Ones? I will not repeat myself, Billy barks at him, you'll come to no good, you pup, mark my words.

Keith nods and tells him no dispute there, he will end up in trouble, very likely with the police. What should he do if they come after him?

I don't have any protection, he points at me, laughing, unlike some, mentioning no names, no Stevie darling to save my hide, isn't that so?

I told Keith about my soldier, and he was all right
about it, even hinting he might like a bit of action in
that quarter, but I didn't take the bait – I'm not sharing
him. So what's your advice to us, sir, should the need
arise? Keith asks Billy. Beastie Billy says, lads, all of you,
not just the smart-arse, you must face facts about your
futures. It's more than a little likely you're all going to
spend a bit of time behind bars. There is not a place
for a squealer to find himself friendless. The rough and
tumble we've all heard tell of in that romper room
might lead to a life permanently on crutches, maybe in
a wheelchair, even confined to a hospital ward dribbling
down your face for the rest of your days. And yet do
you know what the strange thing is, boys? No one
needed to ask him what is the strange thing.

You can have the best of times inside, he smiles.
No worries about paying for grub, even if it tastes
desperate. Clean clothes, clean bed. Decent amount of
sports. Exercise in the gym. Good mates who always
looked after their own. But do you know what is the
best thing about the prison?

No one needed to ask him what is the best thing.

No smell of women. Be at your ease. No scent. No
perfume nor fancy soaps and shampoo to send a man
mad. I instinctively find they dirty a place, ladies do. No
matter how much you scrub a chair after one's sat on
it, the stink of their arses cannot be obliterated. Try as
you might to disguise it, I can still tell within a minute
if a woman has been in a room. I've had that gift for
as long as I've had my first wank. The good thing is
I've learned to control it. Nobody looking at me would
think how often I have had to rush for a toilet – it is the

reason I never wed. Marriage would be a life sentence in the shithouse. Remember that, lads, should you ever be tempted to stray. Don't be afraid either to show your face at Church or Mission Hall. Remember what we stand for as decent Protestants – cleanliness, order, industrious living. Learn to raise your heart in prayer through Christ to God. The people that pray are an invincible people. Work with the lawful authorities to crush the spirit of rebellion without mercy. Be prepared for the day of battle to come.

Keith asks me, well, are you prepared? What are you doing tonight? I say I'm doing nothing.

Good, he says, very good. Make yourself useful tonight. I want you to see my girlfriend. I'm not sure I can, I say.

Why not? Are you jealous or what?

I just can't, I say, I have to see a man about a dog.

What kind of dog? he asks. An army dog?

It might be, but I'm under orders to say nothing, I tell him.

Then don't, he tells me.

8.

Music.

They're sitting on the grass. I see her and him but they don't see me because I've positioned myself in such a way behind a hut that even if they wanted to set eyes on me they couldn't. The sun's going down but it's still shining in my eyes. She is wearing a red shirt and black trousers. He is wearing his nice black T-shirt with a red fist clenched on it and long white shorts I like him to wear.

The last time he was wearing them I was rubbing the calves of his legs and he was saying he liked that, keep doing it, keep on doing it.

Now Keith is with a girlfriend. He does not have his arm around her. His feet are not near her as he's sprawled on the grass not that close to her. He is not kissing her. I'm not saying she is wild-looking or ugly, but I am a bit surprised. She has long hair and I always thought Keith liked short hair. I didn't know what she would be like – I thought she might look like a young fella – but it doesn't matter. My heart is just sore looking at them. I do not want to be his girlfriend, honest to God that's true, but still and all I would like to be where she is with my Keith, for he is mine.

They don't have much to say to each other, for a girl walks past them with a blue cardigan tied around her waist, it falls off, and his girlfriend must have called out something, because the one who's lost the cardigan, she stops in her tracks, looks back, turns and picks it up from the ground. She must be saying thanks and going on her way. That's when Keith sits up. I see he's laughing at something he's said and she starts laughing as well. I wonder what was it they found so funny. Some private joke I will never know what, something only they share.

They put their heads together. They still don't kiss. They must be whispering into each other's ear. Maybe repeating the joke. She puts her fingers into his eyes. She kisses Keith's eyes. She's sucking the sight out of him. She is blinding him. I can see that fucking witch telling Keith he has a girlfriend. Her. He kisses her on the mouth, in the mouth. She has him now, not me.

The tears are tripping me. I've never cried as hard as this. I wish I could stop. But I can't for ages. Ages and ages, and ages. There's nobody there to notice it. I see him the next day.

He says, you didn't show last night. You didn't meet the girlfriend. He asks me where I was.

I say, sorry to disappoint you, I was on business.

Secret business? he asks. Private business? Was he good to you, Stevie? I tell him I can't say, and I really can't. Well, I wait, for things are getting – they are getting – getting a bit out of hand, but I can't say – I just can't.

9.

Music.

I feel like an eejit strapped like this, but it's not sore around my wrists. My arse is bare to the air and I'm bent over but it's Steve who has me like this and I'm not scared of him ever.

He's told me he's not alone tonight. There will be another chap. This man is a higher rank than Steve. We have to call him Sir. Steve says not to call him Steve tonight. Just call him soldier. He asks if I am all right. I tell him, I am, soldier. He then does something he's never done before. He puts a blindfold on me. He says it's for security. See no evil, hear no evil, speak no evil.

I hear the door open. Somebody's come in. Steve's voice changes totally, talking to whoever is there. It gets more swanky. Is this our friend? the other man asks.

Yes, Sir, I hope you approve, Steve replies.

I do entirely – is he from the reliable source?

He is, indeed, and he is a trustworthy citizen of Gomorrah.

Loyal I think you mean, loyal to a fault, loyalists one and all. Now, pretty fellow, be kind to me and I will be very kind to you, Sir tells me.

I can feel Sir's fingers in my short hair. They itch across my scalp. He gives one of my ears a little tug. Then he pulls harder on the other one.

Did that hurt?

No, Sir, not much.

You Irish boys, you're brave little teddies.

I'm not Irish, I'm British, I correct him.

This is when I get the first lash of his cane. It is not across my arse. It is across my face. The shock of it has me squealing, nearly falling on the floor. He gives me another one, where I can't say for sure, because the pain darts everywhere.

He says, we decide who's British, my lad. Wouldn't you agree with me on that, soldier? I hear Steve's voice. It's nearly back to normal after the shock of where the cane landed. He says, this is a good lad, Sir. He does not cause trouble. He is, as you asked for, a loyal fellow.

They are loyal only to themselves.

A lash on the arse. This is a breed that butters us up and destroys us. Another lash.

He stands there with his trousers down expecting a hard fuck.

The cane must be scarring me between the cheeks of my hole.

Then the little bastard expects us to pay him.

Sir is lifting skin off my flesh.

Look at the ridiculous state of him.

I nearly faint with the final blow of the cane.

Clean him up and throw him his money. I'm disappointed in your choice, soldier. I can hear Steve say he's sorry.

Don't be sorry, Sir instructs him. This breed do not understand what sorry means. He was sent here on a mission, and the little coward flinches from doing his duty. What do we pay him for – to blubber like a girl? He's weak, soldier, we've chanced on a bad lot. I can tell from the look of him he might even dare to make allegations. There's no chance he would do that, Sir, Steve assures him.

I don't have your faith in these boys, Sir tells him, they come from vermin, and they'll stay as vermin, no matter how well the likes of you might want to treat them. Warn him – make no allegations. We know who does what – who says what in these parts. We have his name, his address – we know how to harm him. How to silence him. Warn him, and get his gib out of my sight.

Steve drove me into the city. I saw the names of the towns we passed, the wee villages, but here's the funny thing, I stopped recognising any of them, they might as well be written in German.

He wanted to know if I needed anything.

He must have been reading my mind for then he asked if I'd like a feed in a restaurant, some sweet and sour pork, perhaps, my favourite.

I shook my head, I couldn't stomach a bite.

I started crying again – I wanted him to hold my hand.

But he didn't. He said he was sorry things got out of order.

I just said that was life. It was what I expected. No worries. And I wiped my eyes. He told me I was very brave.

I said I wasn't. I just took it for granted Sir didn't like me. I told Steve that's the way it was with me and men. My father, the fucker, did a runner when he looked at me in the cot. Keith was off with his girlfriend. Steve's boss beat shit out of me. What's wrong with me? Will I only want men who don't want me? Am I that wild-looking, Steve?

Steve wanted to know what did I mean about being wild?

I said, in Belfast it meant ugly. Am I ugly, Steve?

He stopped the car. He kissed my forehead.

He said, you're anything but – whoever told you otherwise –

I said, I told myself.

He said to stop doing that. You're going to find a lovely boy who will make you feel like a million dollars. But maybe you should leave Belfast. Maybe it's not the place to stay.

What have I to keep me here? I ask.

Exactly, what have you?

Keith, but it's dawning on me he only wants a girlfriend. Anything in a skirt rather than me or what I can offer him.

And what have you to offer him? Steve asks.

My heart, I say, and the word chokes me, for I've never spoken a truer word. My heart, my heart.

Neither of us say anything, until Steve starts up the car again.

Leave him behind you, he says. He doesn't deserve you. Do a runner. Do it now. Let this help you on your way.

He starts to take money from his wallet.

I say, I've been paid. I don't want your money.

He says nothing, but pushes it into my hand.

I'm sorry I spoke because he looks ashamed.

He tells me to heed Sir's warning well and never breathe a word of what I went through tonight.

What worse could he do me?

No answer out of him to that. So I push it.

A bullet through the head – could they do that?

They could, Steve lets me know, through both our heads.

And I look at his manly face, imagining it clotted with blood, blasted to smithereens, slain by his own kind, not the fucking IRA, and I want to kiss him, now and for all time, but I don't.

I say, I know this is the last time likely I'll see you, so I will be brave and ask you straight out. Steve, you asked me if I wanted anything? I want something, more than anything. This night – just once – can I call you Daddy?

He said no.

10.

Music.

Ma is sober the next time I see her. She's clean as a whistle. She's on the dry – for the time being. She's cut her hair. She's dyed it blonde. She's wearing a nice coat, knee length, brown. She has a darker brown dress on. The only sign she was ever mad are her shoes. They're bright yellow. And her stockings – they're yellow as well. Saffron, that's how she describes them. Cost a pretty penny.

She's sitting in her favourite lounge bar. She's watching racing on television, sipping a mixture of grapefruit and pineapple juice, cursing every one of her many losers. Her pal, Bertha Jones, my godmother, is with her. Bertha is built like a sparrow but can down pints of Harp Lager like the docker all the men in her family were.

Ma always says she's never seen Bertha drunk. Bertha reminds Ma she herself was too drunk to see anybody else drunk, stupid fucker. My mother's favourite story is how once when she was standing on a bridge over the Lagan, singing yoo-hoo, look at me, I'm a canary, Bertha hauled her back from flying off the edge and killing herself. I should have pushed you, Bertha tells her, you cause more bother than you're worth.

There they are, quiet as you like when I see them. Here's your son and heir to your millions, Bertha announces when I walk in. She admires my blue shirt, neatly pressed, more than Ma ever did for me. They teach everything in that home – the best of everything. He didn't know what an iron looked like before they sent him there. Now I'd say it's never out of his hand. Useful to know, I admit, she says, but I hope they're not making even more of a woman out of him. What would you know about being a woman? Bertha accuses her. She asks me if I'd like a drink. I say gin and tonic. She says, maybe your mother's on target, that's a wee girl's drink. My mother says, let him drink like a wee girl – it'll make up for you drinking like a man.

Bertha goes to the counter to order the drink.

You'll never guess what I got this morning, Mammy says.

She produces a letter.

It was delivered to my mother's house. Your Aunt Sandra who still lives there managed to get it to me. It's from your father. He's living in Fermanagh. Doing well for himself. Running boats up and down Lough Erne. Thriving. Teeming with people from all over the world coming to see the lakes, in Fermanagh, forgetting there's still a war in Northern Ireland. Any road, he wants to see the two of us. Wants to know if you'd like to give him a hand running the business. The trollop he abandoned us for, she's done a runner, surprise, surprise. The only shock is it took her so long. Maybe he's lonely. He has no other children. What do you think? Will we go to see him in Enniskillen? It might help me to stay sober –

Is there money in it? I ask. In the letter.

No, she says, not a penny.

Then I say fuck you, Mother.

Then I say fuck you, Father.

Fuck you. Fuck you.

Yes, fuck you – yet, and yet he appears to me, my father, feet lapping through Lough Erne in dreams, in my dreams.

He looks like I remember him, before he left us.
As I think I remember – placing his lean face in a photograph of their wedding day, one she tore to bits in temper, but I still see it.

His face. And if I had forgotten that, I remember his voice.

I could not mistake his voice, singing to me, sitting on his knee, where I am a child, his child, my absent father, my singing father.

And for some reason he is singing about home – home not Fermanagh nor Belfast but home, millions of miles away, somewhere I have never seen nor ever been, but it was a lullaby, him soothing me to sleep, me who never sleeps.

He sings.

The moon shines bright on my Old Kentucky Home,
'Tis summer and people are gay,

The corn-top's ripe and the meadow's in the bloom,
Where the birds make music all the day.
Weep no more, my lady,
Oh weep no more today.

We will sing our song
For my Old Kentucky Home,
For my Old Kentucky Home, far away.

He speaks.

So far away, quite forgotten. My father.

My mother.

My self.

He sings.

Weep no more, my lady,
Weep no more today.

He speaks.

Time to stop weeping.

But ask, why Kentucky? Why fuck ye? Fried Kentucky,
fried chicken, fuck ye Old Kentucky, fuck ye all.

Time to get far, far away.

For in my dream I shed tears for all was done and
cannot be undone, for all was gone, gone, gone, when
I was a child.

One time, I must have been a child.

He sings.

Hard times comes a-knocking at the door,
Then my Old Kentucky Home, good night.

11

Music.

So you're going, Keith says, that's a surprise.

Aye, I'm going.

Where are you heading to?

Anywhere out of this fucking place.

Have you told them in Gomorrah?

What business is it of theirs? I've done my bit for the cause. They've had their money and my hole. I'm quitting while I'm still ahead.

Did you not enjoy being a little boy for the Brits? Was it not your pleasure?

Getting the arse ripped off me? A pleasure? The only time I ever enjoyed it was with you, Keith.

But I'm not a homo.

We slept together.

I can't recall that.

We fucked each other.

I don't remember a thing, funny that, isn't it?

It was in your parents' bed.

Have you been to my house?

I've met your father – he has a hook for a hand.

That's a wee joke we play on strangers.

He lost it driving a taxi.

My old man – a taxi? I don't think so – he can't drive.

This is a wild way to say goodbye.

I'm wishing you all the best.

You're a lying toerag.

About being a homo?

Keith, you were my boyfriend.

No, I wasn't. You wanted me to be. I told you – no.
It's against God's law. Did you never read the bible
foisted on us in Gomorrah? Do you not recall what was
hammered into us?

I'm sure you don't either, I challenge him.

But I do, he tells me, and so should you. Beware of all
abominations in the sight of the Lord. Come to my side,
the side of the Protestant prophets. Your enemies shall
fall before you by the sword. For I will establish my
covenant with you, and I will cut off the names of the
idols and they shall be no more remembered, for the
mouth of the Lord has spoken it.

He burst out laughing.

He says, haven't I been blessed with a great memory?
And yet I have no recollection of the sin you claim
we committed. Strange that, is it not? By the way, it
might be advisable not to mention such matters. Beastie
Billy and his cohorts, the net really is tightening on
them. They'll be facing a long stint off the streets of
our province. Weren't you the lucky boy you stuck to
servicing Stevie and his merry men?

I look into his face. It's hardened from the face I used to love. I start to see it ageing, a bit of fat on the cheek, a rough line on the forehead, hair thinning a little at the right side of the scalp, red starting to colour and disfigure his beautiful skin.

I would like that face to be an egg, so I could smash it, but then I would drink the mess, raw, yellow, pus. I would devour it in one go, choking on the shell.

I turn on my heel and leave.

He says nothing.

If I looked back, I'd lay down my life for him, so I don't.

I tell myself I must move.

I must leave this joint.

I am caked in salt, a pillar of salt, the smell of all my sins.

All I confess to him, though he denied me.

All I relish about him, all that will in time turn my stomach.

All I leave behind.

Ta-ra, ta-ra, ta-ra, ta-ra.

Never to return.

And I have not done so.

I have never glanced back.

I have no need to.

But here's the rub, as they say – here's what shocks me –
what I cannot shake from me. I recognise my breed
when I come across them.

Men who look as though they have seen a ghost, men
who did their bit for Ulster, as I did. I ask them the
same question.

Do you come from Gomorrah?

They nod, as I nod.

Gomorrah, they smile, yes, Gomorrah.

Gomorrah.